Malaria Telediagnostics Us

Nixon Amuomo

Malaria Telediagnostics Using Artificial Intelligence Techniques

Scholar's Press

Imprint

Any brand names and product names mentioned in this book are subject to trademark, brand or patent protection and are trademarks or registered trademarks of their respective holders. The use of brand names, product names, common names, trade names, product descriptions etc. even without a particular marking in this work is in no way to be construed to mean that such names may be regarded as unrestricted in respect of trademark and brand protection legislation and could thus be used by anyone.

Cover image: www.ingimage.com

Publisher:
Scholar's Press
is a trademark of
International Book Market Service Ltd., member of OmniScriptum Publishing Group
17 Meldrum Street, Beau Bassin 71504, Mauritius

Printed at: see last page
ISBN: 978-613-8-82500-5

Preface

Effective containment and management of diseases outbreaks require reliable diagnosis of the patients and a trained physician to interpret the data in order to give a guided treatment. In many developing countries such as Kenya, bringing these two components together, that is, reliable data and trained physicians has been a tremendous challenge.

The main objective of this book is to demonstrate a prototype of an artificial intelligence (AI) content based image retrieval system (CBIR), using the structured systems analysis and design methodology (SSADM). The system is capable of capturing and matching medical images from digital sources and computing similarity index for pattern matching to provide negative and positive results. Using Oracle 10g database technology, a pattern comparison of the raw gathered images will be stored and compared with a bench marked known image using artificial intelligence techniques (AI).

Though the CBIR system's scope does not include clinical trials, the system demonstrates the possibility of computerizing the diagnosis of major diseases that may require discerning human eye through microscopic observation or digital medium visualization. Using a USB microscope, the captured images of a patient blood sample can be download into a computer for evaluation through this intelligent content-based pattern matching application. The CBIR provides diagnosis result within a few seconds that can be delivered via the mobile phone short messaging service (SMS) system, online and on the computer screen with minimum pathologist intervention.

Table of Contents

List of Tables

List of Figures

Chapter 1: Introduction

In Kenya, many people lose their lives due to late diagnosis of diseases such as malaria. This can be attributed to some extent, lack of proper diagnosis and lack of enough expertise at the source. It is therefore the intention of this project to bridge this gap and use an automated pattern matching application of specimen images. The use of mobile technology will further enhance telediagnosis initiatives.

A simple microscope becomes one of the most basic powerful tools in medical practice since it is the tool used for microscopy observations for diagnosis. It requires a well-trained physician to provide effective diagnosis and treatment recommendations. Conversely, an automatic recognition of an image content is largely unsolved problem. The amount of electronically available visual data grows every day with limited automatic categorization and retrieval of visual data that can help users trying to compare visual information from large image databases.

We take an example of a family doctor located on a remote place who performs an X-ray on his/her patient, but does not have a radiologist to interpret the image. A CBIR system will help the doctor in his/her assessment by viewing and comparing the X-ray images to help in knowing the possible ailments of the patient. This tele-microscopy will drastically reduce both the cost and time of performing critical disease diagnosis in resource constrained setting like Kenya.

Chapter 2: Literature Underpinning

Since its inception, mobile phones have become indispensable in people's daily life essentially for ease and immediate communication needs. Various phone manufacturers have been offering attractive features on various phone models in order to position themselves in the competitive market, which is growing steadily worldwide each year. Nowadays mobile phones mean much more than just simple voice communication devices, they are used for data exchange and as data capture tools. With all the user-friendly features the "Smartphone" term is used more frequently to imply the robust functionalities of the mobile phones. Providing multimedia capabilities has been one of the biggest improvements in this field with various phone camera providing multimedia capturing, browsing, editing, and sharing (e.g. via MMS multimedia messages) features in the market.

Camera phones have been widely adopted by people, and thus accelerated digital multimedia generation and sharing with increasing computer, digital camera, and Internet usage. Presently there is huge amount of distributed digital multimedia available for personal and commercial use in the market. An average camera phone user may even possess a large multimedia collection stored in memory cards. However, accessing and finding certain multimedia items within has been quite a challenge.

Perennial diseases are prevalent in Kenya leading to sizable morbidity and mortality. Early and accurate diagnosis of the nature of parasites has always been made with a microscope, which is essential and crucial for appropriate choice of remedial drugs. Many patients are at a high risk with either false negative or false positive diagnosis of diseases due to lack of professionals in the rural areas. Microscopic diagnosis by careful examination of a well-stained blood smear still remains the gold standard for most diseases. However, the expertise and meticulousness needed for such microscopic diagnosis is not widely available, particularly in remote areas and rural areas. It is the intention of this project to tap from this domain and transmit the digitized image to a pattern matching application for diagnosis as opposed to sending the image to a doctor for the same diagnosis.

Oracle multimedia content-based retrieval concepts has been driven by several factors such as communications power of the medium, the commoditization of media capture devices, the standardization of data formats, and the emergence of media capable web page authoring tools and browsers. Multimedia objects are large, unstructured and complex in nature, very different from traditional business data. They come with challenges such as storage and bandwidth costs that can be prohibitive. Oracle meets these challenges by adding support that enables it to manage and deliver image, audio, and video data in an integrated fashion with other enterprise data.

Oracle extensibility framework is a set of unique services that application developers can model into complex logic and extend the core database services, including query optimization, indexing, and SQL, to meet the specific needs of an application. Oracle uses these unique services to provide a consistent architecture for the rich data types and uses object types called ORDImage, ORDAudio, ORDVideo, ORDDoc, and have attributes and methods associated with them.

Searching and matching technology are features in Oracle content-based retrieval concept. Given an image, content-based retrieval technique provides the ability to search images stored in a database table for other images using specific visual attributes such as color, texture, shape, and location.   Content-based retrieval system processes the information contained in image data and creates an abstraction of its content in terms of visual attributes. Any query performed is therefore dealt with solely as an abstraction rather than as with the image itself. Any image inserted into the database is analyzed, and a compact representation of its content is stored in a feature vector, or signature.

The signature for the image in is extracted by segmenting the image into regions based on color. Each region has associated with it color, texture, and shape information. The signature has a region-based information along with global color, texture, and shape information to represent the attributes for the entire image. The images then will be matched based on the color, texture, and shape attributes. The positions of these visual attributes in the image are represented by a location. The image signature contains information about, color, texture, shape and location.

Color

Color is one of the primary components of image analysis for the purpose of content-based image retrieval. Color that is visible to the human eye represents a small range of the entire electromagnetic spectrum that represents everything from cosmic rays to x-rays to electric waves.

Color models - there are several models for representing color. For example;

- **RGB** - Red, Green, Blue; The additive primary colors. Used for monitor screens and most images file formats. There are actually a number of RGB color spaces such as sRBG, Adobe RGB 1998, Bruce RGB, Chrome 2000, etc. differing from each other in the purity of their primary colors, which affects their gamut- the range of colors they represent.

- **CMY(K)** - Cyan, Magenta, Yellow; The subtractive primary colors: the compliments of the additive primaries (Cyan is red, magenta is green; yellow is blue.)
- **HSV** - Hue, Saturation, Value. Hue is what we perceive as color. S is saturation: 100% is a pure color. 0% is a shade of gray. Value is related to brightness. HSV and HSL (below) are obtained by mathematically transforming RGB. HSV is the identical to HSB.
- **HSL** - Hue, Saturation, Lightness. H is the same as in HSV but L and V are defined differently. S is similar for dark colors but quite different for light colors. Also called HLS.

The Electromagnetic Spectrum

The color wavelength visible to the human eye ranges from 4000 to 7000 angstroms. This is similar to an electromagnetic radiation with wavelengths between about 380 and 700 nanometers. This radiation is known as *light*. The visible spectrum and electromagnetic radiation are illustrated below. Color visible to human eye represents a small range of the entire electromagnetic spectrum representing everything from cosmic rays to x-rays to electric waves.

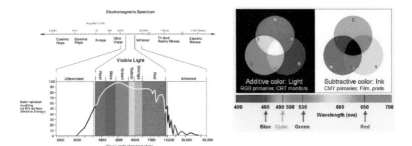

Figure 1: The Electromagnetic Spectrum

This represents the colors violet and red and all of the colors in between. All other waves ranging from cosmic rays from the stars to the FM waves to our radios cannot be perceived by the human eye. It is this small range of the spectrum that is referred to as human perceived *color spaces.*

Color Spaces - Describes human perception of color differences. The two primary color spaces are CIE and HSV models which are the typical color spaces used in content-based image retrieval systems.

Commission International de L'Eclairage (CIE) Color Model

The CIE color model was developed by the French Organization Commission International de L'Eclairage in early 20th century. The model is based on the tristimulus theory of color perception, in which three different types of color receptors in our eyes, the cones, respond differently to different wavelengths of light. The response differential between the three cones can be represented in a 3-D model as per below.

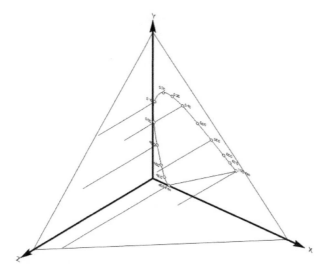

Figure 2: Three dimensional CIE model - Z coordinates projected to the XY plane

The below representation is that of the above 3-D model projected onto a 2-D graph

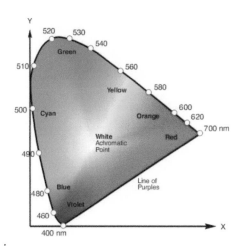

Figure 3: CIE color model mapped to X and Y coordinates

From the figure w above, the CIE color model represents the wavelengths (400nm or 4000 angstroms for violet to 700 nm or 7000 angstroms for red) of human visible light. The color white comes about when all three cones are stimulated evenly. Despite CIE model being a very precise method to measure color, it is not a very practical nor easy method to use to examine color. *Therefore, many current CBIRS utilize the **HSV** color space for image analysis.*

Hue, Saturation, Value (HSV) Model

This model represents color in its distinct components of hue, saturation, and value.

Hue – These are a set of primary colors that when combined together creates all other colors within the visible human spectrum. The primary colors are red, green, and blue same as computers primary colors. Equal mixing of these colors produce what is known as the secondary colors of cyan, magenta, and yellow.

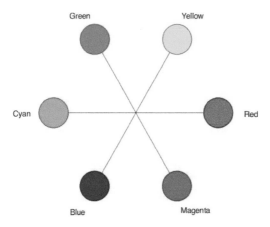

Figure 4: Primary and Secondary Color Wheel

As the mixing goes on, inter-mixing colors will produce tertiary, quandary etc. and eventually produce a solid ring of colors. The definition of color based on the combination of primary colors is called *Hue*.

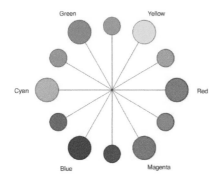

Figure 5: Primary, Secondary, and Tertiary Color Wheel

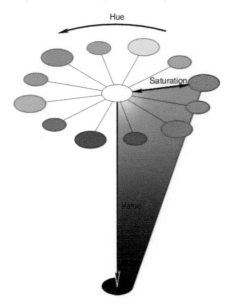

Figure 6: Hue, Saturation, and Value Color Wheel Model

Saturation and Value

Figure 6 above shows saturation that means the dominance of a particular hue within a color. If color is less saturated, is it closer to white and the more saturated color is, closer it is to the pure color found on the outer edge of the HSV color wheel diagram (toward the pure colors). The value of a color is the intensity (the lightness or darkness). While the two components appear to be similar, they have different effects concerning the visibility of a color. Figure 7 also shows that a highly saturated color will have a lower value as noted from the red color. A highly valued color will have less saturation and a color closer to black. And minimally saturated means minimal valued color will be white. HSV model utilizes its components of hue, saturation, and value to quantify a color, which is easier and that's why many CBIRS utilize this method for color analysis.

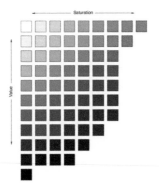

Figure 7: Comparing Saturation and Value within HSV model

Color Representation

The models are used to quantify colors. For example, the CIE-RGB model (the color model for computer monitors per the CIE color model), has some numeric values for each color component: R – Red, G – Green, B – Blue such as R:60, G:10, B:20. The same can be found in the HSV model in which numeric values are assigned to individual colors for the hue, saturation, and value.

The image having been composed of many pixels, meaning many small segments that when put together piece together the image like a puzzle. It is then necessary to find a way to represent the numeric representation of color for the thousands of pixels that make up an image.

In determining the image similarities, content based retrieval system uses **color histogram**. Color histogram represents an image by breaking down the various color components of an image and graphs out the occurrences and intensity of each color like the graphs below. Therefore, to compare two images, one needs only to now compare the color histograms of the two images and determine the similarity of the two histograms.

Color Histogram

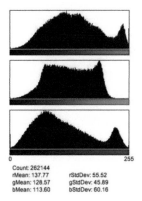

Count: 262144
rMean: 137.77   rStdDev: 55.52
gMean: 128.57   gStdDev: 45.89
bMean: 113.60   bStdDev: 60.16

Figure 8: Color Histogram diagrams

Figure 8 above is a histograms break down of an image by noting its red, green, and blue components. To compare two images, you need compare the color histograms of the two images and determine the similarity of the two histograms.

Color Correlogram

This method of comparison does not take into account of space information. That is, the space or distance between one color vs. another color, but solves the issue of integration of spatial information into color histograms.

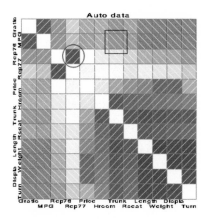

Figure 9: Representation of a color correlogram

It is also known as scatterplots, correlograms will create a visual representation of the image as in figure 9. While the histogram will note the number of colors and their intensities, a correlogram will be able to note space information indicating the distance between the different colors. Therefore, when comparing two different images, it is not only the color components that are being compared, but also the distance they are from each other. Correlograms are more stable when color changes, large appearance changes, and contrast and brightness changes.

Effects of light on pictures

The eye has three classes of color-sensitive light receptors called *cones*, which respond roughly to red, blue and green light (around 650, 530 and

460 nm, respectively). A range of colors can be reproduced by one of two complimentary approaches:

Additive color: Combine light sources, starting with darkness (black). The *additive primary* colors are red (R), green (G), and blue (B). Adding R and G light makes yellow (Y). Similarly, G + B = cyan (C) and R + B = magenta (M). Combining all three additive primaries makes white.

Subtractive color: Illuminate objects that contain dyes or pigments that remove portions of the visible spectrum. The objects may either transmit light (transparencies) or reflect light. The *subtractive primaries* are C, M and Y. Cyan absorbs red; hence C is sometimes called "minus red" (-R). Similarly, M is -G and Y is -B. The two approaches are illustrated on the right and described in the table 1 below.

Table 1: Additive and subtractive approaches

Additive color	Subtractive color
Light sources: beams of light or dots of light on monitor screens	Objects that transmit or reflect light: film or prints. Typically illuminated by white light.
Primaries: Red (R), Green (G), Blue (B)	Primaries: Cyan (C), Magenta (M), Yellow (Y)
Light from independent sources is added.	Portions of the visible light spectrum are absorbed by inks, which contain

	dyes or pigments, or by dye layers in photographic film or paper.
Adding red and green makes yellow (R + G = Y); Similarly, G + B = C and R + B = M. Adding all three additive primaries in roughly equal amounts creates gray or white light.	Each subtractive primary removes one of the additive primary colors from the reflected or transmitted image. Cyan (C) removes red; hence it is known as minus red (-R). Similarly, M is -G and Y is -B. Objects are typically illuminated by white light. Combining two subtractive primaries makes an additive primary (see illustration). Combining all three subtractive primaries in roughly equal amounts creates gray or black.

A wide range of colors can be obtained, but not *all* the colors the eye can see, by combining RGB light.

It is not practical to use RGB or CMY(K) to adjust brightness or color saturation because each of the three color channels would have to be changed, and changing them by the same amount to adjust brightness would usually shift the color (hue). HSV and HSL are practical for editing because the software only needs to change V, L, or S. Most of the image editing typically transforms RGB data into one of these representations, performs the adjustment, then transforms the data back to RGB.

The models of human perception of color differences are described in the form of color spaces. A content-based image retrieval system uses these color spaces. An image is composed of many pixels or many small segments that when put together piece together the image. Oracle content based image retrieval then represents the numeric representation of color for the thousands of pixels that make up the image.

Texture

Texture analysis is another key component of the image. That is, the perception of smoothness or coarseness of an object. Similar to the color histogram, many of the current techniques for image texture analysis, lack the spatial information allowing one to compare the location of a coarse object within an image vs. a smooth object. Some of the texture image analysis and classification methodologies are discussed below and *Gabor filters*.

- **Tamura features** – This breaks out texture features into components such as coarseness, contrast, directionality, line likeness, regularity, and roughness designed in accordance with psychological studies on the human perception of texture. Wold features discussed below handles the first three concepts.

- **Simultaneous Auto Regressive Model (SAR)** - This model is an instance of Markov random field (MRF) models, which is successful in texture modeling in the past decades. Compared with other MRF models, SAR uses fewer parameters with the SAR model taking pixel intensities as random variables.
- Others are **Multi Resolution Autoregressive Model (MRSAR)**, shift-invariant principal component analysis (SPCA) and Tree-Structured Wavelet Transform (TWT) (J. Mao, A.K. Jain, Vol. 25, 173-188, 1992)
- **Gabor Filters** - Gabor functions when applied to images convert image texture components into graphs similar to the ones below.

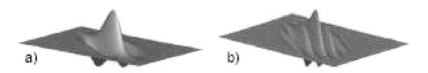

Figure 10: Gabor Filter Representation of Image Texture – a, b

The careful manipulation of these Gabor filters will allow one to quantify the coarseness or smoothness of an image. For example, within the above figure 10 (b) could indicate a coarser texture than that of what was found in figure 10 (a). The comparison of the images is performed against the mathematical representation of the graphs. This enables content based image retrieval systems to compare the textures of two different images.

Wold Features - Similar to Gabor filters, Wold features utilizes a mathematical function and coefficients to represent the texture of an image. The Wold decomposition algorithm breaks down image texture into the components of *periodicity, directionality*, and *randomness*. As noted in Liu and Picard, these three components correspond to the dimensions of human textual perception determined by a psychological study. Figure 11 below shows the Wold method has better precision than other traditional texture methods.

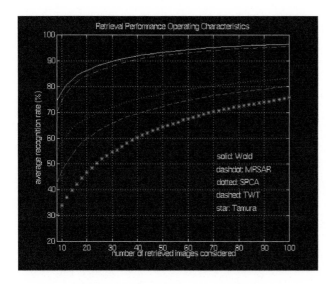

Figure 11: Wold features for texture comparison vs. other methods

Wavelet Decomposition – This algorithm converts image information into a graph or some mathematical representation that can be quantified. Wavelet transformation provides a multi-resolution approach to texture analysis and classification. They are already used in various forms of image analysis such as:

- Wavelet analysis is largely monotonic. meaning it lacks the ability to analyze color information within its transform.

- The wavelet transform is able to transform both scale and frequency information into a simpler mathematical representation. Most algorithms are able to only transform scale information.
- A study by Georgetown University Radiology department showed that the usage of Daubechies Wavelet had the highest compression co-efficiency with lowest mean square error when analyzing digital mammograms. That meant extremely efficient compression and low error rate when analyzing the image.

The wavelet transform processes an image via its horizontal and vertical edges separately and is able to separate low frequency and high frequency information for both sets of axis. That is to say from individual objects within an image and edges, noise etc.

Shape

Shape features are usually described after the images have already been segmented or broken out. A good shape representation of an image should handle changes in translation, rotation, and/or scaling. This is rather difficult to achieve as the images involve numerous geometric shapes that when numerically characterized, will typically lose information.

Oracle image matching process ensures that signatures are generated for the actual image and each new image to be compared with it. Images are seldom identical, and therefore matching is based on a similarity-measuring function for the visual attributes and a set of weights for each attribute. The score is the relative distance between two images being compared. The score for each attribute is used to determine the degree of similarity when images are compared, with a smaller distance reflecting a closer match.

On the other hand, matching works by assigning an importance measure, or weight, to each of the visual attributes, and oracle calculates a similarity measure for each visual attribute. Each weight value reflects how sensitive the matching process for a given attribute should be to the degree of similarity or dissimilarity between two images. For example, if you want color to be completely ignored in matching, assign a weight of 0.0 to color; in this case, any similarity or difference between the colors of the two images is totally irrelevant in matching. On the other hand, if color is extremely important, assign it a weight greater than any of the other attributes; this will cause any similarity or dissimilarity between the two images with respect to color to contribute greatly to whether or not the two images match.

Weight values can be between 0.0 and 1.0 and during processing, the values are normalized such that they total 1.0. The weight of at least one of the color, texture, or shape attributes must be set to greater than zero. **Score:** The similarity measure for each visual attribute is calculated as the score or distance between the two images with respect to that attribute. The score can range from 0.00 (no difference) to 100.0 (maximum possible difference). Thus, the more similar the two images are with respect to a visual attribute, the smaller the score will be for that attribute.

As an example of how distance is determined, assume that the dots in figure 12 below represent scores for three images with respect to two visual attributes, such as color and shape, plotted along the x-axis and y-axis of a graph.

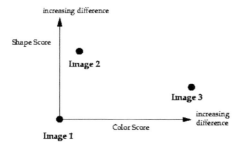

Figure 12: Score and Distance Relationship

As an illustration for matching, assume Image 1 is the comparison image, and Image 2 and Image 3 are each being compared with Image 1. With respect to the x-axis and y-axis, the distance between Image 1 and Image 2 is relatively small whereas the distance between Image 1 and Image 3 is much greater. Thus when images are matched, the degree of similarity depends on a weighted sum reflecting the weight and distance of all three of the visual attributes in conjunction with location of the comparison image and the test image. Again whether or not the two images are considered matching depends on the threshold value. If the weighted sum is less than or equal to the threshold, the images match. If the weighted sum is greater than the threshold, the images do not match.

Another way in which oracle content based retrieval does matching is by using an Index to compare signatures. It does this through a domain index, or extensible index which is an approach for supporting complex data objects. This index is of type ORDImageIndex and once it is created, the index automatically updates itself every time an image is inserted or removed from the database table. The index will be created, managed, and accessed by routines supplied by the index type. This application uses a fuzzy search engine, and is not designed to do correlations. For example, the application will not find a specific vehicle in a parking lot. However, if the car image is cropped from a picture of a parking lot, we can then compare the car to known car images.

Global Image Transformations

A common methodology is to utilize the wavelet transform which transforms the entire image into frequency components that can be quantified and compared against. With respect to shape, this may be problematic because all information (color, texture, shape) are encoded and hence not possible to differentiate the differences based solely on shape. It is not possible to compare some part of an image. So many CBIR systems that perform shape characterization by the use of global image transforms, presume that each image contains only a single shape.

Boundary Based – by attempting to identify boundary of a particular image, many boundaries based shape characterizations exist. Information such as color and texture often help in the identification of the boundaries as well.

Some examples are; Rectilinear shapes, Polygonal Approximation, Finite Element Models and Modal Matching / Fourier-Based Shape Descriptors.

These various methodologies try to trace out the actual image and thus able to identify the shape. The identified shape is then compared to stored identified shapes and the same procedure is carried out on other images to be compared.

Region Based – Region based shape characterizations is also referred to as a statistical moments of an image. The concept of moment (mathematics) evolved from the concept of moment within physics according to Wikipedia. The latter concept illustrates the magnification of force in rotational system between the application of force and where the force is applied. The concept borrows from Newton's second law of inertia, that says an object in motion continues in that same motion unless acted upon by some external force. The law states that the acceleration of an object is proportional to the force exerted on that object. The constant of proportionality is also called inertial mass represented by the M in figure 13 to 19 below

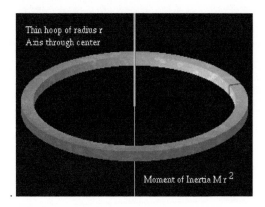

Figure 13: Moment of Inertia (thin hoop)

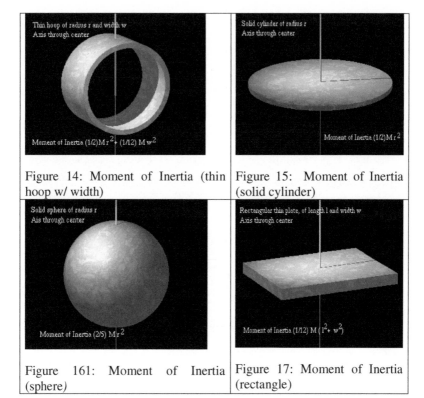

| Figure 14: Moment of Inertia (thin hoop w/ width) | Figure 15: Moment of Inertia (solid cylinder) |
| Figure 161: Moment of Inertia (sphere) | Figure 17: Moment of Inertia (rectangle) |

Thin hoop of radius r and width w
Axis through center

Moment of Inertia $(1/2)Mr^2 + (1/12)Mw^2$

Solid cylinder of radius r
Axis through center

Moment of Inertia $(1/2)Mr^2$

Solid sphere of radius r
Ais through center

Moment of Inertia $(2/5)Mr^2$

Rectangular thin plate, of length l and width w
Axis through center

Moment of Inertia $(1/12)M(l^2 + w^2)$

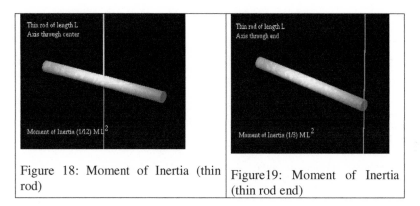

Figure 18: Moment of Inertia (thin rod)	Figure 19: Moment of Inertia (thin rod end)

When force is applied to rotate an object, the angular acceleration is linearly proportional to the force, and its constant of proportionality is called the *moment of inertia*. The above diagrams depict how this relates to shape and pattern recognition. You will notice that the images while having the same height, weight, and radius, have different moments. This means that, different shapes have different formulas and have different numerical values for their moments even though they share the same characteristics.

Mathematically, moments can be described as the *nth* moment of a real valued function *f(x)* of a real variable is:

$$\mu'_n = \int_{-\infty}^{\infty} x^n f(x)\, dx.$$

That implies that, moments seek to characterize sequences of values (1, 2, 3, ...), specifically sequences of values derived from the above formulae

Multimedia Content Storage

The application captures images and stores them in the form of Binary large objects (BLOBs) with is stored locally in Oracle transaction control. They can contain audio, image, or video data. The media data can also be stored outside the database, without transaction control. In this case, a pointer is stored in the database under transaction control, and the media data is stored in:

- File-based large object (BFILE)
- An HTTP server-based URL
- A user-defined source on a specialized media data server, or other server

Media data stored outside the database can provide a convenient mechanism for managing large, existing or new, media repositories that reside as flat files on erasable or read-only media. This data can be imported into BLOBs at any time for transaction control and will require loading of the multimedia data into a database.

This project entirely involves integrating online uploading of images into a pattern matching application database system via wireless communication system as its signal capturing device. It involves transmission of pathological images to a database from a mobile phone using a wireless medium and internet.

Image Compression Methods (Tradeoffs and comparisons)

Compression algorithms are: **lossy** and **lossless**. Lossy means that the decompressed image isn't losses some of the information, but only information that is judged to be insignificant is left. While *lossless* means they preserve all the original information.

TIF

- RGB - 24 or 48 bits, Grayscale - 8 or 16 bits, Indexed color - 1 to 8 bits, Line Art (bi-level)- 1 bit.
- Most programs allow either no compression or LZW compression (lossless, but is less effective for 24-bit color images).

PNG

- RGB - 24 or 48 bits, Grayscale - 8 or 16 bits, Indexed color - 1 to 8 bits, Line Art (bi-level) - 1 bit.
- PNG uses ZIP compression which is lossless, and slightly more effective than LZW (slightly smaller files).

JPG

- RGB - 24 bits, Grayscale - 8 bits.
- JPEG always uses **lossy** JPG compression, but its degree is selectable, for higher quality and larger files, or lower quality and smaller files.

GIF

- Indexed color - 1 to 8 bits.
- GIF uses lossless LZW compression, effective on indexed color.

Tradeoff for using each image format

Table 2: Tradeoff for using each image format

	Photographic Images	**Graphics, including Logos or Line art**
Properties	Photos are continuous tones, 24 bit color or 8 bit Gray, no text, few lines and edges	Graphics are often solid colors, up to 256 colors, with text or lines and sharp edges
For Unquestionable Best Quality	TIF or PNG (lossless compression and no JPG artefacts)	PNG or TIF (lossless compression, and no JPG artifacts)

Smallest File Size	JPG with a higher Quality factor can be decent.	TIF LZW or GIF or PNG (graphics/logos without gradients normally permit indexed color of 2 to 16 colors for smallest file size)
Maximum Compatibility (PC, Mac, Unix)	TIF or JPG	TIF or GIF
Worst Choice	256 color GIF is very limited color, and is a larger file than 24 bit JPG	JPG compression adds artifacts, smears text and lines and edges

Table 3: Tradeoff for using each image extension file

Format	Extension	Compressed or uncompressed	Lossy or lossless	Geo-aware?	Suitable for large images?	Proprietary or open?
BBB	.bil, .bip, .bsq	Uncompressed	Lossless	Yes. (somewhat)	Yes	Open
GeoTIFF-raw	.tif	Uncompressed	Lossless	Yes	Yes. up to 2GB	Open
GeoTIFF-LZW	.tif	Compressed	Lossless	Yes	Yes. up to 2GB	Open
PNG	.png	Compressed	Both	No	No	Open
GeoTIFF-JPEG	.tif	Compressed	Lossy	Yes	Yes. up to 2GB	Open
IPG	.png	Compressed	Lossy	No	No	Open

The goal of data compression is to represent the data in a way that reveals some redundancy. We may think of the color of each pixel as represented by a three-dimensional vector *(R, G, B)* consisting of its red, green, and blue components. In a typical image, there is a significant amount of correlation between these components. For this reason, we will use a *color space transform* to produce a new vector whose components represent *luminance, Y,* and blue and red *chrominance, C_b* and *C_r.*

$$\begin{bmatrix} Y \\ C_b \\ C_r \end{bmatrix} = \begin{bmatrix} 0.29900 & 0.58700 & 0.11400 \\ -0.16874 & -0.33126 & 0.50000 \\ 0.50000 & -0.41869 & -0.08131 \end{bmatrix} \begin{bmatrix} R \\ G \\ B \end{bmatrix}.$$

Figure 20: Color Space Transform

The luminance describes the brightness of the pixel while the chrominance carries information about its hue. These three quantities are typically less correlated than the *(R, G, B)* components.

Since this transformation is invertible, we will be able to recover the *(R, G, B)* vector from the *(Y, C_b, C_r)* vector. This is important when we wish to reconstruct the image. (To be precise, we usually add 128 to the chrominance components so that they are represented as numbers between 0 and 255.) When we apply this transformation to each pixel in our block, we obtain three new blocks, one corresponding to each component as shown figure 21 below. The brighter pixels correspond to larger values.

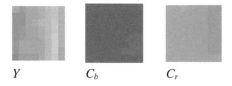

Y $\qquad$ C_b $\qquad$ C_r

Figure 21: Color Space Transform – three new blocks

As is typical, the luminance shows more variation than the chrominance. For this reason, greater compression ratios are sometimes achieved by assuming the chrominance values are constant on 2 by 2 blocks, thereby recording fewer of these values. Digital images such as photographs are generally encoded as rows and columns of *pixels* (from *pic*ture *el*ements). This type of image format is called a raster image. The more pixels in each row and column, the better the *resolution* of the image. An image with 24 bits of color information for each pixel will generally look better than an image with only 16 bits of color information for each pixel. Again, the better the color resolution, the bigger the image file.

Image compression algorithms are designed to minimize image file size in order to speed up image data transmission.

Image Quality and Artifacts

Two costs of compression are performance and artifacts. Compressed files may take longer to process (e.g., color balance, further compress, etc.) or decode (e.g., decompress, view, etc.). And compression can introduce visible patterns, anomalies or distortions in an image that weren't present in the original data.

Common types of artifacts are mosaic (i.e., an image composed of two or more joined images or "tiles") might display seam lines as an artifact of the mosaicking process or tonal imbalances caused by differences in the weather conditions under which each tile was photographed. These are image-level artifacts not related to compression. Compression artifacts are caused by the mathematical algorithms used to compress images. Different compression algorithms leave different artifacts.

Chapter 3: Artificial intelligence in health - Overview of k-Nearest Neighbor

Nearest neighbor learning is one of the most popular instance based learning methods. Other instance-based learning methods include locally weighted regression and case-based reasoning methods. Another related method is Radial Basis Function (RBF) networks which are a type of artificial neural network constructed from spatially localized kernels. The approach to learning of these methods differs from other learning methods. Many learning methods construct a general explicit description of the target function when training examples are provided. In contrast, learning in these algorithms is seen as consisting of simply storing the presented training data. Then when a new query is presented, a set of similar related instances is retrieved from memory and used to classify the new query instance.

Many of these techniques construct a local approximation to the target function that applies in the neighborhood of the new query instance encountered, and never construct an approximation designed to perform well over the entire instance space. This has an advantage when the target function is very complex, by describing it as a collection of less complex local approximation. Nearest neighbor and locally weighted regression methods assume that instances can be represented as points in a

Euclidean space. They are conceptual methods that can be used to approximate real-valued or discrete-valued target functions.

Locally weighted regression is a generalization of k-nearest neighbor in which an explicit local approximation to the target function is constructed for each query instance. Here the local approximation to the target function can be based on a variety of functional forms such as constant, or linear, or quadratic functions, or on spatially localized kernel functions.

k-Nearest Neighbor learning

The k-nearest neighbor algorithm makes the assumption that all instances correspond to point in the n-dimensional space ^{n}. This is illustrated in Figures 1, 2 and 3 using a 2-dimensional classification task. The two classes here are "x" and "o" with eight examples for each class. A query point (or instance) x_q, is then presented and the nearest neighbors are used to classify it.

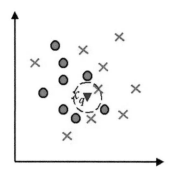

Figure 22: 1 Nearest neighbor.

This classifies the query point x_q as a member of the "x" class. When $k=1$, the 1 nearest neighbor makes a rather unstable classifier (high variance and sensitive to data).

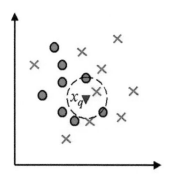

Figure 23: 3 Nearest neighbors.

This classifies the query point x_q as a member of "o" class, since there are 2 "o" and 1 "x" class neighbors.

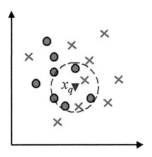

Figure 24: 7 Nearest neighbors.

This classifies the query point x_q as a member of "o" class, since there are 5 "o" and 2 "x" class neighbors.

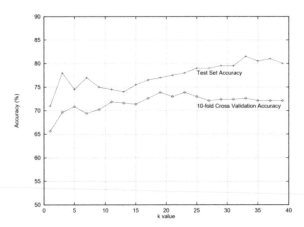

Figure 25: The value of k against the 10-fold cross validation and test set accuracy

This is used to select the best value of k, in this case, either 19 or 23. This reduces the variance, but may increase the bias as there is averaging. Because of the Bias-Variance trade-off, the best way of choosing the value of k is by plotting cross validation classification accuracy against k.

Figure 25 depicts the general relationship between the value of k and the 10-fold cross validation and testing accuracy. Generally, the cross validation accuracy is initially low with a small k value, but as k is increased, the accuracy increases to some value, then reduces and evens out in this case for the range of k we have used. Theoretically we expect the accuracy to increase with an increase in the value of k.

For a closer look at k-nearest neighbor algorithm, let an arbitrary instance x be described by the feature vector

$$< a_1(x)a_2(x), \cdots\cdots a_n(x) >$$

where $a_r(x)$ is used to denote the values of the rth attribute of instance x. If we consider two instances x_i and x_j, then the distance between them is defined as $d(x_i, xj)$, which is expressed in Equation 1.

$$d(x_i, x_j) \equiv \sqrt{\sum_{r=1}^{n} (a_r(x_i) - a_r(x_j))^2}$$

The K-nearest Neighbor Classification

The nearest neighbor classification is one in which a new pattern is placed in the class to which it is closest as shown in figure 26 below.

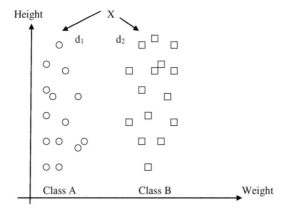

Figure 26: The nearest neighbor classification

Legend: ○ - Ballet dancer   ○ - Rugby player

   d_1 is the shortest distance to class A

   d_2 is the shortest distance to class B

   X is the unclassified pattern

Consider a discriminant function f(X), where f(X) = closest (Class A) – closest (Class B).

If f(X) is positive, then place in class B.

If f(X) is negative, then place in class A.

In practice, all (k) members are taken into account. In this case we have k-nearest neighbor, where k is the number of samples. A general problem is to find a reliable measure of distance from one class of samples. There are several k-nearest neighbor methods that are discussed below.

The Hamming Distance

Let $X = (x_1, x_2, x_3, \ldots, x_n)$ and $Y = (y_1, y_2, y_3, \ldots, y_n)$ be any two input vectors, then the hamming distance between then denoted by H is given by:

$$H = \sum_{1}^{n} |x_i - y_i|$$

The hamming distance is commonly used to compare binary vectors where it gives the number of different bits. Note that $|x_i - y_i| = x_I \text{ XOR } y_I$.

The Euclidean Distance

When applying *k*-nearest neighbor algorithm, the distance between instances is calculated on *all* attributes of the instance. In other words, all axes in the Euclidean distance containing the instances are considered. An important point to note here is that this is in contrast to other machine learning algorithms such as rule and decision tree learning systems that select only a subset of the instance attributes when forming a hypothesis.

This is an accurate distance metric based on Pythagoras's theorem. It is defined as given below.

Let $X = (x_1, x_2, x_3, \ldots, x_n)$ and $Y = (y_1, y_2, y_3, \ldots, y_n)$ be any two input vectors, then the Euclidean distance between then denoted by $d(X, Y)_{euc}$ is given by the below formulae and depicted in figure 27.

$$d(X,Y)_{euc} = \sqrt{\sum^{n} (x_i - y_I)^2}$$

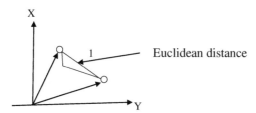

Figure 27: The Euclidean distance

When input vectors are binary, the Euclidean distance is the square root of the Hamming distance. The amount of computations is reduced by approximating Euclidean distance using the net methods that are faster but less accurate.

The City-Block distance

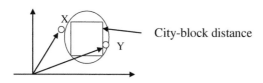

Figure 28: The City Block distance

Let $X = (x_1, x_2, x_3, \ldots, x_n)$ and $Y = (y_1, y_2, y_3, \ldots, y_n)$ be any two input vectors, then the City-block distance between them, denoted by d (X, Y) $_{cb}$ is given by:

[55]

$$d(X,Y)_{cb} = \sum_{1}^{n} |x_i-y_I|$$

No square roots are taken.

The Square Distance

Let $X = (x_1, x_2, x_3, \ldots\ldots, x_n)$ and $Y = (y_1, y_2, y_3, \ldots\ldots, y_n)$ be any two input vectors, then the Square-block distance between them, denoted by $d(X, Y)_{sq}$ is given by:

$$d(X, Y)_{sq} = \max\{ |x_i-y_I|\},$$

where the maximum value of the differences (or the longest side) is taken.

Chapter 4: Methodology - System Design and Implementation

The standard software development life cycle model (SDLC) was used as a software development methodology process for the CBIR system using Oracle technology integrated with SMS Gateway and web servers' configurations.

The CBIR system was designed using the Structured Systems Analysis and Design Methodology (SSADM).

SSADM was adopted as a technique because it offers the following advantages.

1. SSADM builds up several different view of the system which is used to crosscheck one another. There are three different views created: -
   - The underlying structure of the system's data (the Logical Data Model).
   - How the system's processes operate and how these interact with data (Data Flow Models, and Conceptual Process Modelling).
   - How the systems data is changed by events over time (Entity Event Modelling, Entity Behavior and Process modelling).

2. SSADM combines techniques into well-established (default) frame works, as well as providing the techniques for the analyst/designer and it gives guidance on how to use them.

3. SADM is an open method. No license fee required for it.

4. Its structured analysis provides a clear statement of requirements that everyone can understand and is a firm foundation for subsequent design and implementation.

5. Has improved project planning and control.

6. Produces better quality systems.

Data flow diagrams (DFD's)

These are graphical tools that enable simple representation of entire system in as small a space as one page. They give a well overall view of what should be regarded as a 'Logical' process, entity external to any of these processes.

Components of a DFD

- **Processes** -are individual functions the system carries out. Inputs transformations into output.

- **Data stores** – a collection of data packets at rest.

- **Flows** – an arrow(s) into or out of a process. Describes the movement of chunks or packets of information from one point of the system to the other.
- **Terminators** – external entities with which the system communicates. (A person or a group).

Entity relationship diagrams (ERDs)

An entity is an instance of an entity type that is uniquely identifiable. It is concerned with data and their relationships.

Components of a ERD's

- **Object types (entity)** –anything in the system under study about which, we wish to store information and which is capable of existing independently.
- **Relationship** – is a meaningful association among entity types.
- **Super type / subtype indicators** – a subtype entity inherits its attributes and its relationships from the super type entity. (Contains unique attributes). A super type (generalization) contains the shared attributes.
- **Attribute** – is a property of an entity or relationship type.

Diagram Conventions

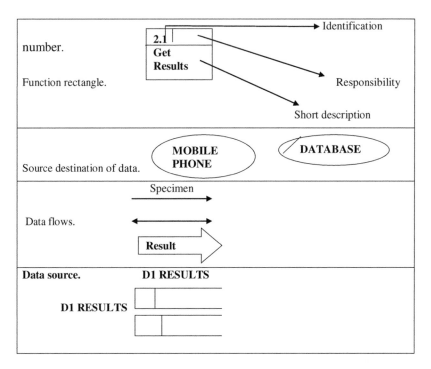

Figure 29: Diagrams Conventions

Application Design Architecture

Database design is the design of a collection of information organized into interrelated tables of data and specifications of data objects.

An overview of system's chart

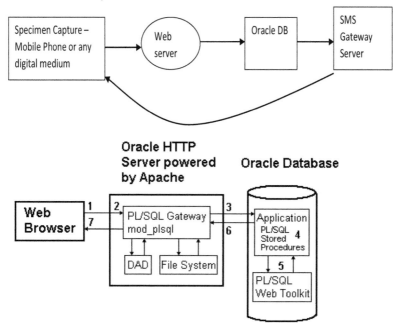

Figure 30: Application design architecture

Process Modelling

SYSTEM: TELEDIAGNOSTIC	DATE:
AUTHOR: NIXON O. A	PAGE: 1

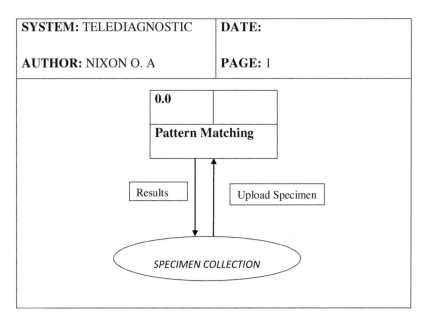

Figure 31: Process Modelling

Data Modelling

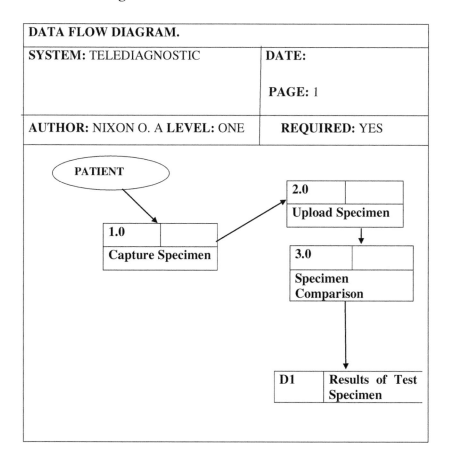

DATA FLOW DIAGRAM.	
SYSTEM: TELEDIAGNOSTIC	**DATE:** **PAGE:** 1
AUTHOR: NIXON O. A **LEVEL:** ONE	**REQUIRED:** YES

Figure 32: Data Flow Modelling

Physical Model

Physical Database design is concerned with file organization and access. The steps adopted for this project are:

- Translation of the global logical data model for the target DBMS (Oracle).
- Designs of base relations – tables, fields, data types the appendix section.
- Design of enterprise constraints – triggers, validations, and error handling and application programs.

Design of security mechanisms - Designed user views and access rules with password encryptions coupled with GSM sim card security rules under administrative access roles.

Chapter 5: Results

Image Compression Algorithms and methods test results.

An Experimental Procedure to test image compression algorithms and methods using this very tool was analyzing for the best image compression algorithm for deployment. To compare the algorithms, an image against itself (skinspecimen1) returns the results as indicated below from various compression methods.

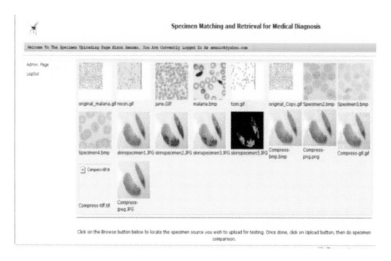

Figure 33 : Uploading specimens page

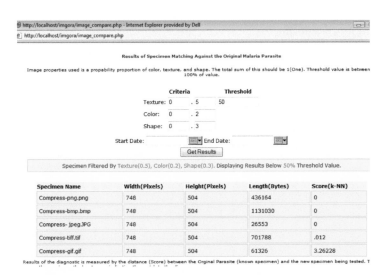

Figure 34 : Uploading specimens for compression algorithms testing

File format	File size
Bmp	1,105Kb
Tiff	686Kb
Png	426Kb
Gif	60Kb
Jpeg	26Kb

Figure 35 : Image compression algorithms and storage (Size)

The CBIR System Walkthrough – Automated Malaria testing

The application has been designed for online access. It has a module for adminsitration tasks. After a health worker or user logs in, they will be able to select which disease they need to diagnosis on as per screen in figure 36.

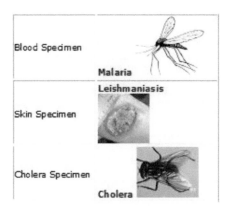

Figure 36 : Menus for disease selection

Browse to select the directory or path where the raw specimen is on your mobile phone or laptop. Ensure you correctly label the specimen with the patient name or id. Then select the specimen and click on upload.

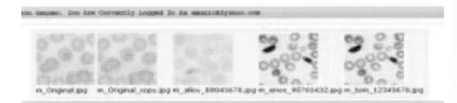

Figure 37 : Sample specimen images uploaded

Once upload is done, an SMS report will be delivered only to the registered health worker or user as shown in figure 38. Alternatively, the results can be accessed online from the web page. Figure 39 shows the message on a mobile phone- *'Specimen result for id_1245_John.jpg, has a core of '0.019' meaning, the specimen closely malaria parasite. Malaria found. - Powered by e-diagnostic*

Figure 38 : Test result message displayed on the mobile phone

Specimen Name	Width	Height	Length	Score	Status
m_Original_copy.jpg	263	247	5203	0	The Specimen Closely Matches the Parasite.
m_alloy_89045678.jpg	256	259	4487	3.63937	The Specimen Closely Matches the Parasite.

Figure 39 : Test results accessed online

The above test results shows two specimens, one marked as original copy (a replica of the identified positive pathogen) and compared to a second specimen from Alloys. The CBIR system using the Euclidean distance (attributes, color, texture, and shape), computed the results as shown in figure 39.

[69]

Chapter 6: Conclusion

Telediagnostics system for use in telemedicine is viable solution that has been demonstrated through this CBIR application. This system has the potential to save lives in areas where health experts are unavailable and leverage on available telecommunication technology and allow a health worker in a remote location, with the aid of a mobile phone, to treat a patient. With faster internet access available this application will be cost effective in meeting the universal health coverage goals for the developing countries. The time taken to reach healthcare will be shortened, laboratory fees, and the transport cost saved can be used on other basic needs by the poor. This technology has also been developed using readily available tools and open source software such as the gateway server and apache server, to further reduce cost of the technology.

Digital media has become a central component of today's online applications. Focus is now turning on how the advent of faster internet and telecommunications services can be used to enhance health. The increase in volume and valuation of various multimedia types has highlighted the importance of managing media objects. Complexity is a factor as well because the management and use of media presents unique problems to each application area.

With Oracle, media data is managed along with other application specific data making both overall management and application development easier. The emerging wireless space also gives an opportunity for development of interactive applications that can be used to bridge the gap between experts and the so called privileged society through rich content information sharing.

Recommendation

"Microscopy is still considered the gold standard" for some diseases diagnosis, says Katherine Herz, a medical doctor and a fellow in health policy at Stanford University and that, "If microscopy could be done with portable equipment, it might be adopted far more widely and prove extremely useful." And that's the motivation for this project.

It is against this remark that we recommend future development of USB microscopes capable of integrating with digital sources to ride on this for telemedicine deployments. More research needs to be done on better image analysis technologies to reduce noise interferences and go an extra mile to have mobile phone fabrications to act as a microscope.

References

1. Telemicroscopy for diseases diagnosis [Online]. (Accessed on 11th Nov. 2017). http://fletchlab.berkeley.edu/research_cellscope.htm.

2. CS Godse, S Patkar, NS Nabar , AJ Amonkar, RA Vaidya, AA Raut, AB Vaidya. *Mobile Camera Microphotography: A Simple But Elegant Technique For Telediagnosis of Malaria.* [Online]. (Accessed on 30th Nov. 2011): http://www.jkscience.org/current/new%20horizons/TELEPHONE.pdf.

3. Richard O. Duda, Peter E. Hart, David G. Stork, "Pattern Classification" (2nd Edition), Wiley-Interscience, edition 2000

4. Gonzalez, Woods. *Digital image processing.* Pearson education. Second edition.

5. Jennifer Dy, Carla Brodley, A. C. Kak, Lynn Broderick, and Alex Aisen, "Unsupervised Feature Selection Applied to Content-Based Retrieval of Lung Images," IEEE Transactions on Pattern Analysis and Machine Intelligence, pp. 373-378, March 2003.

6. Chi-Ren Shyu, Christina Pavlopoulou, A. C. Kak, Carla E. Brodley, and Lynn S. Broderick, "Using Human Perceptual Categories for Content-Based Retrieval from a Medical Image Database," Computer Vision and Image Understanding, Vol. 88, Number 3, pp. 119-151, December 2002.

7. Efrain Turban, David King/Denis, *Electronic commerce, a managerial perspective* 2006

8. N. Kasitipradith, *The Ministry of Public Health telemedicine network of Thailand. International Journal of Medical Informatics*, Volume 61, Issue 2 - 3, Pages 113 – 116

9. Matthew Gast, *Wireless Networks*: The Definitive Guide, Publisher: O'Reilly Pub Date: April 2002 ISBN: 0-596-00183-5 Pages: 464

10. Stuart Russell and Peter Norvig. Artificial Intelligence: A Modern Approach. Prentice Hall, 1995. available at http://www.aima.cs.berkeley.edu.

11. http://tie.telemed.org/articles/article.asp?path=telemed101&article=se curenetwork_ef_tpr03.xml accessed on 12/04/2018

12. J. Mao, A.K. Jain, Texture classification and segmentation using multi-resolution simultaneous autoregressive models, Pattern Recognition, Vol. 25, 173-188, 1992

Appendix

Sample codes - A script for comparing images

```php
<?

session_start();

if(!isset($_SESSION['logged_in']))

{

  //header('Location: ./script/redirect.php');

  echo "You Session Has Expired, Please Log In Again!";

  exit;

}

?>

<!DOCTYPE html PUBLIC "-//W3C//DTD XHTML 1.0 Transitional//EN""http://www.w3.org/TR/xhtml1/DTD/xhtml1-transitional.dtd">

<html xmlns="http://www.w3.org/1999/xhtml">
```

```html
<head>

<link href="./resources/template1.css" rel="stylesheet" type="text/css"/>

<script language="javascript" src="script/numbersOnly.js"></script>

<script language="javascript" src="script/threshold_values.js"> </script>

<script language="javascript" src="script/default_vals.js"></script>

</head>

<body class="white_bg" onload="return defaults()">

<p align="center"><b><font color="#800000">Results of Specimen
Matching Against the Original Malaria Parasite</font></b></p>

<p align="center"><font color="#000000">Image properties used is a
probability proportion of color, texture, and shape. The total sum of this
should be 1(One). Threshold value is between 1-100% of
value.</font></p>

<table align="center" width="95%">

  <tr>

    <td>
```

```html
<form name="select_criteria" method="post">

<table align="center">

  <tr>

    <th colspan="4">Criteria</th>

    <th>Threshold</th>

  </tr>

  <tr>

    <td>

      <label>Texture:</label>

    </td>

    <td>

<input type="text" name="texture" id="texture" onKeyPress="return numbersonly(event, false)" onkeyup="return get_totals()" size="4">

    </td>

    <td>.</td>
```

```html
<td>

<input type="text" name="texture1" id="texture1" onKeyPress="return
numbersonly(event, false)" onkeyup="return get_totals()" size="4">

</td>

<td><input type="text" name="threshold" id="threshold"
onkeypress="return numbersonly(event, false)" size="12" /></td>

</tr>

<tr>

<td><label>Color:</label></td>

<td>

<input type="text" name="color" id="color" onKeyPress="return
numbersonly(event, false)" onkeyup="return get_totals()" size="4" />

</td>

<td>.</td>
```

```
<td><input type="text" name="color1" id="color1" onKeyPress="return
numbersonly(event, false)" onkeyup="return get_totals()" size="4"
/></td>

    <td>

    <input type="submit" value="Get Results" name="submit"
onClick="return max_num()" />

    </td>

    </tr>

    <tr>

    <td><label>Shape:</label></td>

    <td>

<input type="text" name="shape" id="shape" onKeyPress="return
numbersonly(event, false)" onkeyup="return get_totals()" size="4" />

    </td>

    <td>.</td>
```

```html
<td><input type="text" name="shape1" id="shape1"
onKeyPress="return numbersonly(event, false)" onkeyup="return
get_totals()" size="4" /></td>

    </tr>

    </table>

  </td>

</tr>

<tr>

  <td colspan="5" align="center">

    <table>

    <tr>

        <td>Start Date:</td>

      <td>

<input class="plain" name="dc1" value="" size="12"
onFocus="this.blur()" readonly /><a href="javascript:void(0)"
onClick="if(self.gfPop)gfPop.fStartPop(document.forms[0].dc1,documen
```

t.forms[0].dc2);return false;" ><img class="PopcalTrigger" align="absmiddle" src="DateRange/calbtn.gif" width="34" height="22" border="0" alt=""></a>

</td>

<td>End Date:</td>

<td><input class="plain" name="dc2" value="" size="12" onFocus="this.blur()" readonly /><a href="javascript:void(0)" onClick="if(self.gfPop)gfPop.fEndPop(document.forms[0].dc1,document .forms[0].dc2);return false;" ><img class="PopcalTrigger" align="absmiddle" src="DateRange/calbtn.gif" width="34" height="22" border="0" alt=""></a>

</td>

</tr>

</table> </form>

<hr align="center" width="100%" color="#003399" />

</td>

</tr>

```php
<tr>

<td>

<?php

/* This Section Retrieves Height and Width Properties Of Images In
The Database */

if(isset($_POST['submit']))

{

include('config.php');

    $thresh = $_POST['threshold'];

    $texture = $_POST['texture'].'.'.$_POST['texture1'];

    $kolor = $_POST['color'].'.'.$_POST['color1'];

    $shape = $_POST['shape'].'.'.$_POST['shape1'];

    $to_date = $_POST['dc1'];

    $from_date = $_POST['dc2'];

    if($to_date!='' && $from_date!='')
```

{

$sql="SELECT Q.IMAGENAME, Q.PHOTO.getWidth() as wdh,Q.PHOTO.getHeight() as hgt,Q.PHOTO.getContentLength() as cnt,ORDSYS.IMGScore(123) SCORE ,CASE WHEN ORDSYS.IMGScore(123) < 20 THEN 'Positive' ELSE 'Negative' END as Status FROM imagesdata1 Q,imagesdata1 E WHERE e.image_id=101 AND Q.image_id != E.image_id AND ORDSYS.IMGSimilar(Q.photo_sig, E.photo_sig,'color=$kolor, texture=$texture, shape=$shape', $thresh, 123)=1 AND q.dates BETWEEN to_date('$to_date','mm/dd/yyyy') and to_date('$from_date','mm/dd/yyyy') Order by ORDSYS.IMGScore(123) ASC";

}

else

$sql="SELECT Q.IMAGENAME, Q.PHOTO.getWidth() as wdh,Q.PHOTO.getHeight() as hgt,Q.PHOTO.getContentLength() as cnt,ORDSYS.IMGScore(123) SCORE ,CASE WHEN ORDSYS.IMGScore(123) < 20 THEN 'Positive' ELSE 'Negative' END as Status FROM imagesdata1 Q,imagesdata1 E WHERE e.image_id=101 AND Q.image_id != E.image_id AND

```php
ORDSYS.IMGSimilar(Q.photo_sig,E.photo_sig,'color=$kolor,
texture=$texture,   shape=$shape',   $thresh,   123)=1        Order   by
ORDSYS.IMGScore(123) ASC";

    }

    $query = oci_parse($con,$sql);

    oci_execute($query);

echo "<p align=center class=highlight><font color=blue> Query Filterd
By </font><font color=red> Texture(". $texture ."), Color(". $kolor ."),
Shape(". $shape ").</font><font color=blue> Displaying Results Below
</font><font color=red>". $thresh ."</font><font color=blue> Threshold
Score.</font></p>";

    echo "<table align=center width=95% border=0>";

    echo "<tr align=left>";

echo          "<tr          align=left          class=highlight><th>Image
Name</th><th>Width</th><th>Height</th><th>Image
Length</th><th>Image Score</th><th>Status</th>";

    while($row=oci_fetch_assoc($query))

    {
```

```php
        echo "<tr align=left>";

echo        "<td        class=highlight>".$row['IMAGENAME']."</td><td
class=highlight>".$row['WDH']."                    </td><td
class=highlight>".$row['HGT']."</td><td
class=highlight>".$row['CNT']."                    </td><td
class=highlight>".$row['SCORE']."</td><td
class=highlight>".$row['STATUS']."</td>";

        echo "</tr>";

        }

        echo "</table>";

        oci_close($con);

    }

?>

    </td>

</tr>

</table>
```

```
<iframe   width=132   height=142   name="gToday:contrast:agenda.js"
id="gToday:contrast:agenda.js"          src="DateRange/ipopeng.htm"
scrolling="no"   frameborder="0"   style="visibility:visible;   z-index:999;
position:absolute; top:-500px; left:-500px;">
```

</iframe> *Results of the diagnostic is measured by the distance (Score) between the Original Parasite (known specimen) and the new specimen being tested. The nearer the specimen, the least score indicating the match to the disease.*

```
</body>
```

```
</html>
```

Tools used

- Internet enabled cell phone.
- Dreamweaver web development.
- Toad for oracle.
- Oracle developer Tools.
- PHP.

Druck:
Canon Deutschland Business Services GmbH
im Auftrag der KNV-Gruppe
Ferdinand-Jühlke-Str. 7
99095 Erfurt